Earth's Changing Continents

by Neil Morris

www.raintreepublishers.co.uk
Visit our website to find out more information about **Raintree** books.

To order:
 Phone 44 (0) 1865 888112
Send a fax to 44 (0) 1865 314091
Visit the Raintree Bookshop at **www.raintreepublishers.co.uk** to browse our
catalogue and order online.

First published in Great Britain by Raintree,
Halley Court, Jordan Hill, Oxford OX2 8EJ,
part of Harcourt Education.
Raintree is a registered trademark of Harcourt
Education Ltd.

Editorial: Nick Hunter and Catherine Clarke
Design: Michelle Lisseter and Bridge Creative
Services Ltd
Picture Research: Maria Joannou and Liz Eddison
Illustrations: Bridge Creative Services Ltd
Production: Jonathan Smith

Originated by Dot Gradations Ltd
Printed and bound in China by South China
Printing Company

ISBN 1 844 21393 5
07 06 05 04 03
10 9 8 7 6 5 4 3 2 1

**British Library Cataloguing in Publication
Data**
Morris, Neil
Earth's Changing Continents. – (Landscapes and
People)
551.4'1
A full catalogue record for this book is available
from the British Library.

Acknowledgements
The publishers would like to thank the following
for permission to reproduce photographs:
Bruce Coleman Collection pp. **12** (Christer
Fredriksson), **19** (Staffan Widstrand); Corbis
pp. **7** (James A. Sugar), **11** (Wild County), **13**
(top) (Lloyd Cluff), **24** (David Turnley), **29**
(Tom Wagner); NHPA pp. **10** (John Shaw), **15**
(Norbert Wu); Oxford Scientific Films (David
Cayless) p. **14**; Rex Features pp. **22** (Sipa Press),
23 (Peter MacDiarmid); Science Photo Library
pp. **5** (Dynamic Earth Imaging), **9** (Worldsat
International), **27** (John Beatty); Werner
Foreman Archive p. **18**.

Cover photograph of fully dark (city lights) image
centred on Europe reproduced with permission of
Marit Jentoft-Nilsen, VAL, NASA GSFC.

The publishers would like to thank
Margaret Mackintosh for her assistance
in the preparation of this book.

Every effort has been made to contact copyright
holders of any material reproduced in this book.
Any omissions will be rectified in subsequent
printings if notice is given to the publishers.

Contents

What is a continent?   4

How did the continents form?   6

Changing landscapes   10

Changing life   14

Changing settlements   18

Changing continents   24

Continent facts and figures   28

Glossary   30

Further reading   31

Index   32

Any words appearing in the text in bold, **like this**, are explained in the Glossary.

What is a continent?

The town or village where you live is part of a county or state. In turn, the county or state belongs to a larger region called a country. Did you know that every country also forms part of an even bigger area, called a continent?

We use the word continent to describe one of the world's main large areas of land. There are seven continents altogether, and some of these huge land masses are connected to each other. In order of size, from biggest to smallest, the world's continents are: Asia, Africa, North America, South America, Antarctica, Europe and Oceania. Australia, together with New Zealand, Papua New Guinea and thousands of small Pacific islands, makes up the continent called Oceania. This continent is sometimes called Australasia.

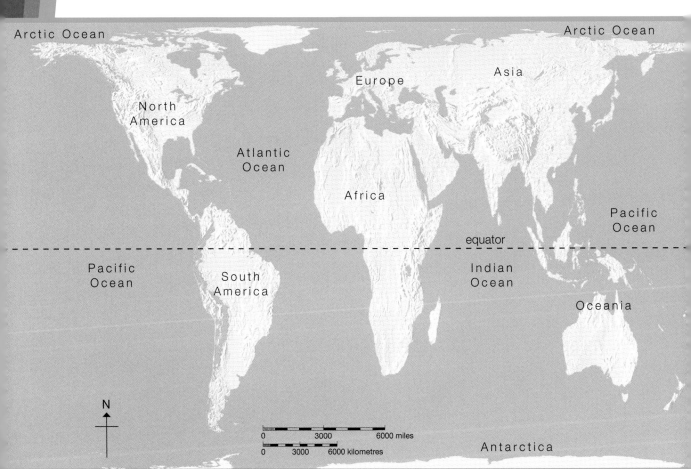

The southern continent of Antarctica is at the bottom of the world map. At the top, the Arctic region is made up of frozen ocean and the most northerly parts of North America, Europe and Asia.

Separated by oceans

Four oceans lie between the world's continents: the Pacific, Atlantic, Indian and Arctic oceans. The oceans are so big that their waters cover more than two-thirds of Earth's surface. The world's largest ocean – the Pacific – is just under four times as big as the world's largest continent – Asia.

Looking at continents

Earth's continents were formed millions of years ago. Since then, they have been constantly, but very slowly, changing. They are home to millions of different kinds of plants and animals. People have tried to control the land they live on, and we continue to change the continents.

This satellite photograph shows the large land mass of Australia. Together with New Zealand, Papua New Guinea and thousands of small Pacific islands, it makes up the continent called Oceania.

Linked continents

Some of the continents are linked. For example, a narrow strip of land (which we call Central America) joins the continents of North America and South America. Together, the continents of Europe and Asia form an even larger land mass, called Eurasia. Europe and Asia are divided by a range of mountains called the Urals. Asia is also linked to Africa by a piece of land called the Sinai peninsula. Large oceans separate the other continents.

How did the continents form?

Scientists believe that Earth came into existence about 4600 million years ago. When it was first formed, the planet was red-hot and the surface was covered with **volcanoes**. The volcanoes let off masses of steam, like a boiling kettle does, and when the steam cooled, it fell back to Earth as rain. There was so much rain that it collected into huge pools that eventually became one big, deep ocean.

Earth's outer layer

Beneath the deep ocean, our planet had a rocky outer layer, which today we call Earth's **crust**. The crust became harder as the planet gradually cooled down. The crust is not one continuous layer, like the shell of an egg or the peel of an orange. It is cracked into huge pieces, called **plates**. Earth's plates fit together like a giant jigsaw, with the two sides of each plate close up against each other.

This map shows the world's major plates. As they move, they change the shape of continents.

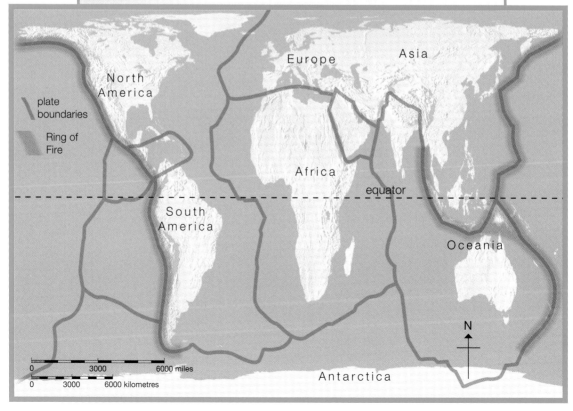

Continental plates

There are two types of plate – continental and oceanic. As their name suggests, continental plates are the ones with dry land on them. They form the continents that we are looking at in this book. The rocks that make up continental plates are very old and were mainly formed over 2500 million years ago. Continental plates are also thick – about 40 kilometres (25 miles) thick on average, reaching up to 80 kilometres (49 miles) beneath high mountain ranges. Oceanic plates make up the **seabed** of the world's oceans. Oceanic plates are younger than continental plates – generally less than 200 million years old. They are also thinner – an average of 10 kilometres (6 miles) thick.

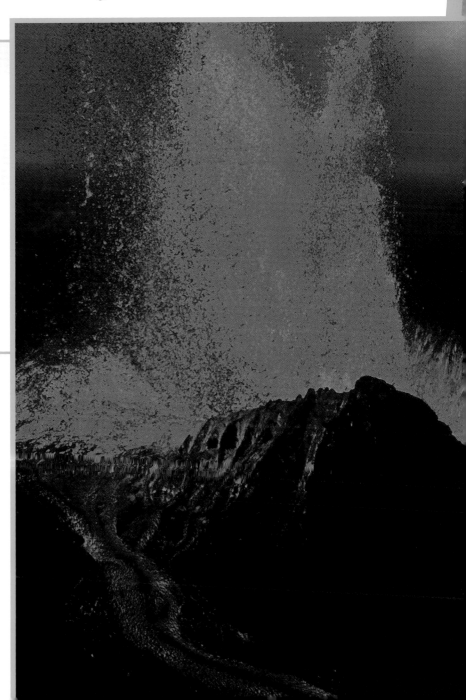

*Beneath Earth's crust the rock is so hot it has melted. At the edge of plates this **molten** rock, called **magma**, sometimes forces its way through an opening in the crust. This makes a volcano.*

Supercontinent

Many millions of years ago separate continental **plates** drifted together and joined up in one piece. The land then formed one huge continent, called a supercontinent. The supercontinent was surrounded by a single ocean. The scientist who discovered this, called the supercontinent Pangaea (from the Greek for 'all earth') and the huge ocean Panthalassa ('all sea').

Drifting apart

Around 200 million years ago, Pangaea split into two continents that began to slowly move apart. Scientists called the northern large continent Laurasia, and the southern continent was called Gondwanaland. Over millions of years, the continents went on splitting until they formed the land masses that we know today. This movement is called continental drift, because the continents

This map shows what the continents looked like around 250 million years ago. Gondwanaland became South America, Africa, Oceania and Antarctica. The land that is now India was once part of the southern continent, but it broke away and drifted to the north, becoming part of Asia.

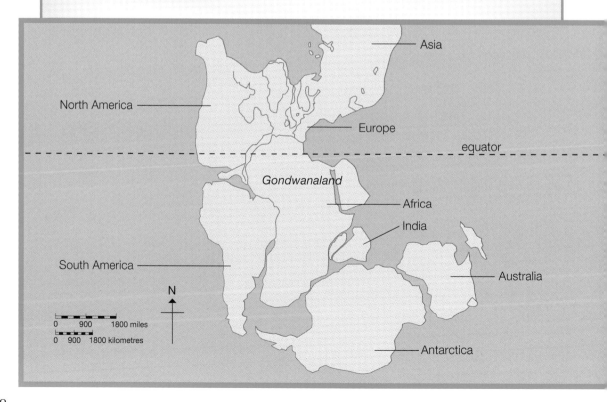

slowly drifted apart. These changes are still going on – for example, North America and Europe continue to move apart by just a few centimetres every year.

Today, the easiest way to see how the continents split apart is to look at the east coast of South America and the west coast of Africa. Can you see how they would fit together again? Today they are divided by the Atlantic Ocean. A huge mountain range, called the Mid-Atlantic Ridge, stretches right down the middle of the ocean. This is where new crust is created, pushing the continents apart.

Moving and scraping

Earth's plates are not still – they are always moving, very slowly, by just a few centimetres each year. Some move towards each other, others move apart, and some move past each other. When they push against each other, the plates buckle (bend) at the edges. It is this action that pushes mountain ranges up. The rubbing action of plates pushing against each other has another important effect. It creates **volcanoes** and **earthquakes**, which mainly occur at the edge of plates. There are mountain ranges on the ocean floor, too, but these are formed in a different way. As two plates move apart, **magma** comes to the surface and cools to form new **crust**.

Changing landscapes

The whole of Earth's hard, solid **crust** is made of rocks. In many places, the rocks that make up the world's continents are covered with soil. This contains tiny bits of rock, as well as the rotting remains of dead plants and animals. In other places, especially high up in the mountains or near the **coast**, there is no soil and the rocks are bare. There are many different kinds of rocks, but they are all made of solid substances called **minerals**. The colour of a rock, as well as its hardness and weight, depend on the minerals in it.

Forming different rocks

There are three main groups of rocks. They take their names from the way in which they are formed. **Sedimentary** rocks, such as sandstone, are made up of layers of sediment (tiny particles of rock). These build up on top of one another and are squeezed together until they harden into rock. Other rocks, such as granite, harden from hot **magma** (see page 7). These rocks are called **igneous** (meaning 'fiery'). The third kind of rocks are called

> Sedimentary rocks are formed in layers, called **strata**. As **plates** move and mountains are forced up, the strata are folded. In the mountains and at the coast, you can often see the exposed strata. They look like wavy lines, as shown here at Wave Rock in Australia.

metamorphic (meaning 'changing form'). These rocks are changed by being heated or squashed. The metamorphic rock called quartzite, for example, is a changed form of sandstone.

The rock cycle

Although we think of rocks as the solid ground beneath our feet, they also change over time. In fact, rocks change in a never-ending cycle. **Volcanoes** throw out **molten** rock, which we call **lava**. The lava cools and hardens into solid rock. Over many years the effects of the weather wear this rock away in a process called erosion. Wind and rain break bits of rock off, which rivers carry to the ocean. There the rock particles settle on the ocean floor, pile up and form layers of sediment that, over time, become new rocks. At the same time, heat inside Earth melts more rocks, which are thrown out by volcanoes. This starts the rock cycle all over again.

The metamorphic rock called marble is a changed form of limestone. Marble is a valuable rock, used in buildings and sculptures. Here, white marble blocks are being cut away at a quarry in Carrara, Italy.

Higher and lower land

Much of the land that makes up the continents is hilly or mountainous. Mountains change little during a single human lifetime, but they change a great deal over thousands and millions of years. Some mountain ranges, such as the Himalayas in Asia, are still being pushed higher. The Himalayan range was formed when the land that eventually became India drifted northwards (see page 8) and finally bumped into Asia. Other mountains are very slowly getting smaller.

The Highlands of Scotland were pushed up more than 300 million years ago. At that time, the land that became Europe was on a separate mass before becoming part of the supercontinent, Pangaea. At one time the Scottish Highlands had high, jagged peaks. Since that time, however, the peaks have been worn away to make more gentle and rounded slopes.

Where land meets sea

All the continents have long coastlines, where the land meets the sea. At the edge of every continent, there is a **continental shelf**, where the water is shallow. Here the **seabed** slopes gently away from the shore. Further away from land and out to sea, the shelf turns into a steeper **continental slope**. Even further out, there is a

> The snowy peaks of the Himalayas tower above this valley in Nepal. The world's highest mountains are in this range.

thick pile of sand and mud called a **continental rise**. Beyond that is the deep floor of the ocean. The whole of the region from land to deep ocean is called a **continental margin**.

When you look out to sea, the water seems to change colour further out. This is because the water is deeper out on the continental shelf.

Great Rift Valley

Near the coast of east Africa, there are a series of deep cracks in Earth's **crust** known as the Great Rift Valley. Altogether the Rift Valley is about 7200 kilometres (4470 miles) long, stretching from Syria in the north to Mozambique in the south. It runs all the way across the boundary between the continents of Asia and Africa. The valley was formed about 30 million years ago by the movement of **plates**. These are still moving today, and scientists believe that in millions of years' time the part of Africa east of the Great Rift Valley may separate from the rest of Africa.

Changing life

Changes in the position of the continents long ago had a great effect on the development of plants and animals. When the continents were all joined together as one single supercontinent (see page 8), land animals could walk all over Earth's land without having to cross any sea. When the supercontinent split up, things were different. Animals spread around the world with the continents. This was how the giant **reptiles** called dinosaurs managed to spread around the world. Dinosaurs dominated life on Earth until they suddenly died out about 65 million years ago.

Cut-off continents

As the continents drifted apart, plants and animals developed in different ways on different land masses. This took place many millions of years ago, long before there were any humans on Earth. Today, Australia provides a good example of separate development.

This large land mass broke away from Antarctica and the rest of Gondwanaland about 50 million years ago. Since then it has been surrounded by sea, and its animals and plants have developed in their own way. When European explorers first arrived in Australia just a few hundred years ago, they were amazed at the wildlife they found. They said it was a land where 'birds ran instead of flying and animals hopped instead of running'.

The spider monkeys of Central and South America are experts at using their tails to hang on to trees.

Kangaroos and koalas

Australia's running birds are emus, which are similar to the ostriches of Africa. The hopping animals are kangaroos, which are the best known of Australia's marsupials. These are animals whose young develop in pouches in their mother's body. There are 60 different kinds of kangaroos in Australia, and most of them are not found anywhere else in the world. Another famous marsupial is the koala. It looks a bit like a grey teddy bear, but it is not really related to bears and is only found in Australia.

Monkeys

The continents of South America and Africa once fitted together. Today, some of the wildlife of the two continents are similar, but not exactly the same. South American monkeys, for example, have their nostrils spaced wide apart, while those of their African cousins are close together. The most interesting difference between the two is that most American monkeys use their tail as a fifth limb, to swing through the trees. African monkeys don't do this.

Different habitats

Scientists divide the world into a number of different kinds of environment or **habitat**. Each has its own collection of plants and animals that have **adapted** to life there. The habitats are greatly affected by the **climate**, or typical weather conditions, of the particular region. Regions close to the **equator**, which runs through South America, Africa and south-east Asia, are hottest. Those nearest the North and South Poles, especially the continent of Antarctica in the south, are coldest. In between these two extremes there are mild regions. The different environments on all the continents are also affected by how high the particular region is above sea level, and how near it is to the **coast**.

This map shows how different vegetation is spread in regions across the continents. Most continents have many of the different types of vegetation. South America, for example, has seven types.

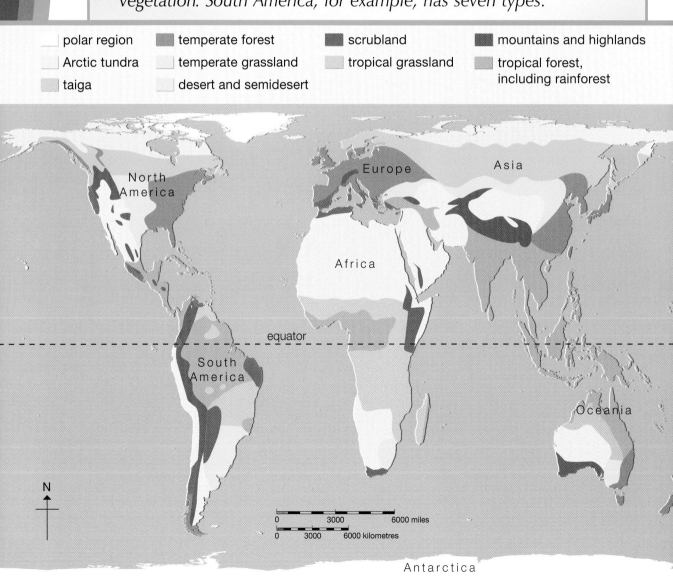

polar region

Arctic tundra

taiga

temperate forest

temperate grassland

desert and semidesert

scrubland

tropical grassland

mountains and highlands

tropical forest, including rainforest

North America

Europe

Asia

Africa

equator

South America

Oceania

N

0   3000   6000 miles

0   3000   6000 kilometres

Antarctica

Life in the tropical rainforest

There are great similarities between the tropical **rainforests** of South America, Africa and Asia. The biggest of them all, the Amazon rainforest of South America, has the greatest number of plants and animals. Scientists believe that up to one-tenth of all the world's **species** of animals and plants may live there, including up to one-fifth of all bird species.

Around the world

Different habitats stretch across the continents in bands (see the map on page 16). You can see this very well if you look at tropical grasslands and **deserts**. One huge forest stretches for 10,000 kilometres (6250 miles) across the northern regions of Europe and Asia, from the Baltic Sea in the west to the Pacific Ocean in the east. This is the world's biggest forest, called taiga (from a Russian word). It continues across North America, covering about half the land area of Canada. North of the forest, in all three continents, is the frozen, treeless Arctic region. To the south are the warmer grasslands of the **steppes** in Russia and the plains in Canada and the USA.

The largest floral kingdom is the boreal (northern) kingdom, which stretches right across North America, Europe, and northern and central Asia.

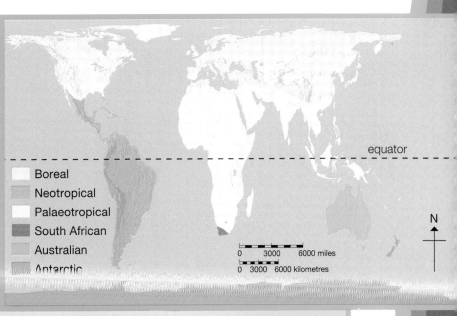

equator

Boreal
Neotropical
Palaeotropical
South African
Australian
Antarctic

0   3000   6000 miles
0   3000   6000 kilometres

N

Floral kingdoms

Flowering plants first appeared on Earth about 140 million years ago, when the continents were drifting apart. They have developed in different ways around the world. Scientists divide the world into six different regions, which are sometimes called floral kingdoms. There have been three main causes for the different regions: the way the continents drifted apart; climate in the past and today; and the way in which individual plants adapted and developed.

Changing settlements

People live on six of the seven continents of the world. The odd-one-out is the frozen continent of Antarctica. Some scientists visit and work there, but no one lives there all the time. Unlike animals and plants, there were no human beings on Earth when the continents split apart many millions of years ago. So how did our **ancestors** manage to **populate** the whole planet?

Out of Africa

Some scientists believe that human-like creatures, called **hominids**, first appeared in east Africa about 6 million years ago. That sounds a very long time ago, but if you imagine the whole of Earth's history as just one day, hominids existed for the equivalent of less than two minutes! Modern humans developed from hominids and appeared in Africa over 100,000 years ago. That's the equivalent of just two seconds ago, when compared with Earth's one day and the hominids' two minutes. Some modern humans travelled north, first to Asia and Europe, and began the movement that finally took people around the whole world.

Scientists have learned a lot about our human history from fossils and bones. Many of these have been found in Africa. This skull was found in Tanzania and is well over a million years old.

The ice age

During the time when humans were moving around the world, the **climate** was very cold. Much more of the world was covered in ice than it is today, and we call that period the ice age. As water turned to ice, sea levels went down around the globe. This meant that people could walk between different land masses. It is thought that the original peoples of Australia, the Aborigines, arrived there around 40,000 years ago. Then the sea levels were lower and there was more dry land, but the earliest people must still have used rafts to cross channels up to 130 kilometres (80 miles) wide.

> *Some Inuit people in northern Canada and Greenland still use kayaks to hunt and fish in a traditional way.*

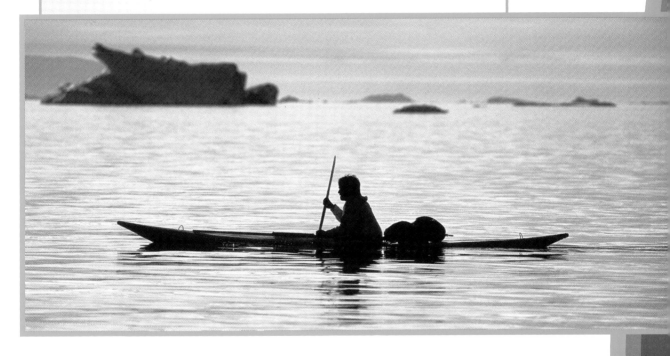

Native Americans

Many scientists believe that the first Americans were hunters from Asia, who crossed the Bering Strait to present-day Alaska about 17,000 years ago. There was then a strip of land between the two continents, which has since been covered by water as ice melted. These people probably stayed near the coast as they headed down towards South America. Some may have followed the course of rivers, knowing that there would always be fish and other animals there to catch and eat. Eventually they spread out across North and South America.

Farming and industry

The world's first people were **hunter-gatherers**. When people started to stay in one place and form **settlements**, thousands of years ago, they became farmers. A few hundred years ago, many parts of the world went through an **Industrial Revolution**, when people began using metals and other **resources** to manufacture (or make) things.

Changing populations

In the last few centuries, the **populations** of different continents have changed rapidly. In 1790, when the first census (official count) was made, the USA had a population of 4 million. Most people had settled near the east coast and along the country's rivers. Since then huge numbers of people have gone to North America from other continents. This is called immigration, and it resulted in the growth of towns and cities, as the USA became an industrial nation. Today, the population is around 280 million and about 2 million of these people are Native Americans. Three-quarters of the US population live in towns and cities.

This map shows the US states, with the number of people living in each one. Two states are not shown: Alaska has a population of 552,000; Hawaii has 1,115,000 people.

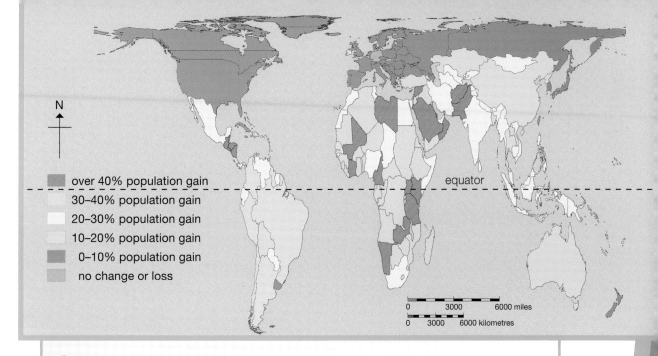

over 40% population gain
30–40% population gain
20–30% population gain
10–20% population gain
0–10% population gain
no change or loss

equator

0   3000   6000 miles
0   3000   6000 kilometres

N

This map shows how population grew across the world in the ten years before the year 2000. North America is interesting. While Canada and the USA had a very low increase, Mexico and the countries of Central America increased rapidly.

The population explosion

Over the last 50 years, there has been a population explosion. In that time the number of people in the world has more than doubled, and is now more than 6 billion. In 1950 less than one-third of people lived in towns. By 2000 the number had grown to almost half, and it is expected to be around two-thirds by 2025. These increases vary across the continents. As you can see from the map above, the population explosion is greatest in Africa. South America and Asia are also high, while Europe is very low, with practically no increase.

Lake Victoria

People settle where there are natural resources to help them with their lives. Water is a precious resource, because it is needed for drinking, washing and watering farmland. Rivers, lakes and seas also have fish in them, which can be caught for food. Lake Victoria is the largest lake in Africa and the third largest in the world. Its shores are divided between the countries of Tanzania, Uganda and Kenya. Millions of people live near the shores of the lake, which they use as an inland sea. Ships link the main ports of Mwanza in Tanzania, Entebbe in Uganda and Kisumu in Kenya.

Living on the edge

Extreme weather can cause natural disasters all around the world, but some continents are in more danger than others. Hurricanes are large, powerful storms with very high winds that cause great damage when they pass over land. They start over warm ocean waters in regions near the **equator**. Atlantic hurricanes mostly affect the Caribbean islands, Mexico and other Central American countries, and the south-east corner of North America. Tropical storms in the Pacific Ocean are known as typhoons (from the Chinese for 'great winds'), and they often hit eastern Asia. In and around the Indian Ocean, these storms are called cyclones.

Floods in Bangladesh

Some regions within continents are at special risk because of their location. The coastal region of Bangladesh, in southern Asia, lies directly in the path of many cyclones that move in from the Indian Ocean. Water also runs off the Himalayan Mountains to this area of flat land around the **delta** of the River Ganges, and it is easily flooded. Almost every year thousands of Bangladeshis are made homeless by floods. In 1998, two-thirds of the country was flooded, claiming around 900 lives and leaving 30 million people homeless.

These Bangladeshi people were among the millions who had to queue for food after they lost their homes in the 1998 flood.

Volcanoes and earthquakes

Volcanic eruptions and **earthquakes** can also cause terrible disasters all over the world. Active **volcanoes** lie at the edge of Earth's **plates** (see page 6), and a large number of them form a huge belt around the Pacific Ocean. This belt is known as the 'Ring of Fire', and earthquakes are very common along its whole length. It affects people on four continents around the world's largest ocean: Asia, North America, South America and Oceania.

> *The town of Bhachau, in north-west India, was left in ruins like these after a powerful earthquake struck in 2001. Tens of thousands of people were killed here and in nearby villages.*

Living on faults

There are thousands of minor earthquakes all over the world every year, but the US state of California has some big earthquakes. They happen because the Pacific coast of California lies along the San Andreas **Fault**, which is 1050 kilometres (650 miles) long. It is the place where two plates are sliding past each other at the rate of about 5 centimetres each year. In 1994 the town of Northridge, 30 kilometres (19 miles) north of Los Angeles, shook for 20 seconds. This earthquake caused the death of 57 people and over 20,000 were left homeless.

Changing continents

Apart from Antarctica, all the world's continents are divided up into countries. In 2003 there were 193 separate countries in 6 continents, but the total number often changes as nations join together or divide. In most continents, neighbouring countries try to help each other, because they face similar challenges. In Europe, for example, many countries are joined together in the European Union, which makes it easier for member countries to trade with each other.

Natural resources

Some of the world's natural **resources** are essential for people's survival. Most of these, including the air that we breathe and the water that we drink, are available on all continents. People's lives have developed in different ways on different continents, however, and there is no longer a balance between the continents. Generally, the northern continents are much wealthier than the southern continents, which allows them to use more of the world's resources, including fresh water. For example, North Americans are generally richer than South Americans, and Europeans are generally better off than Africans. Many of the world's aid agencies are working hard to help the poorer nations. They are trying to make sure that every continent has basic standards of food, housing and education.

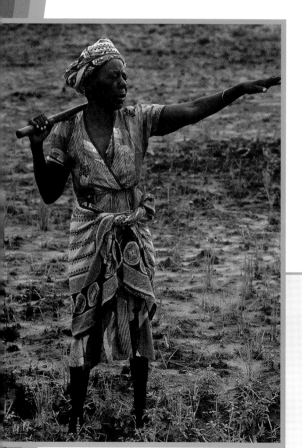

This woman is farming in Tanzania, east Africa. On average, people in Tanzania, have to pay more than 5 per cent of the wages they earn for the fresh water they need every day. In Europe and North America, people pay much less than 1 per cent for their fresh water.

Oil

Oil is one of the world's most important natural resources. It is used to power factories and cars, as well as to make plastics and many other products. There are known oil reserves on all the world's continents, and oil has been a very useful resource to some of the poorer nations in South America and Africa. The first oil well was drilled in Pennsylvania, USA, in 1859. More than 80 years later, oil was discovered beneath the Arabian Desert, in south-west Asia. The discovery brought wealth to the region, and its largest country, Saudi Arabia, is the world's leading producer of crude oil. Scientists have estimated that more than half the world's oil reserves are in this **desert** region.

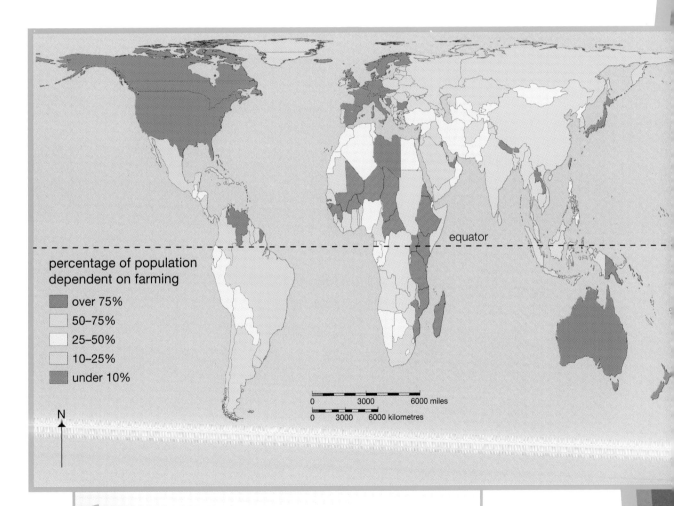

percentage of population
dependent on farming

- over 75%
- 50–75%
- 25–50%
- 10–25%
- under 10%

equator

N

| 0 | 3000 | 6000 miles |

| 0 | 3000 | 6000 kilometres |

This map shows the importance of farming in today's world. Many people are dependent on farming in Africa and Asia, while fewer people are in North America, Europe and Oceania.

The changing climate

Generally the world's **climate** is heating up, by a very small amount each year. Many scientists believe that the warming is partly caused by the greenhouse effect, which is created by heat-trapping gases. These allow heat through to Earth from the Sun, but trap it there, like the glass of a greenhouse. The gases we release by burning fuel, such as the exhaust fumes given off by cars, add to this effect. It may cause a general increase in temperature, called global warming. In turn, this may make the land drier and even cause **deserts** to spread.

Rising sea levels

Many scientists believe that ice at the North and South Poles is melting, because the global temperature is rising. Eventually this will mean that sea levels will rise around the world. This will change the shape of the coastlines around all the continents, flooding existing land near the shore.

> *This map shows how the world's coastlines might change if all the ice at the North and South Poles melted.*

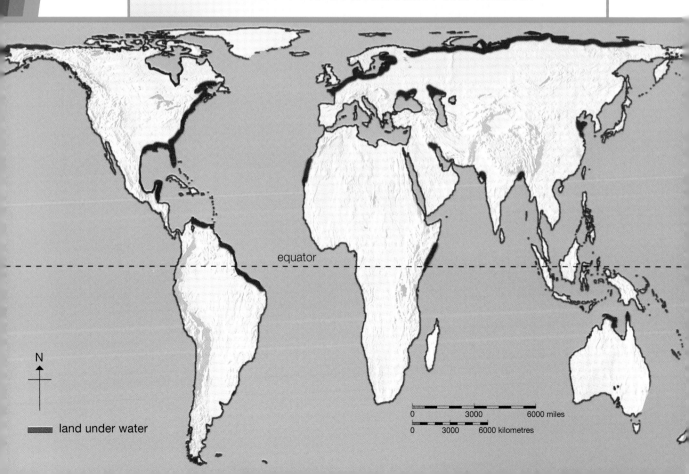

equator

N

0   3000   6000 miles

0   3000   6000 kilometres

■ land under water

Scientists from around the world gather together at the Amundsen-Scott research station at the South Pole, in Antarctica. At the most southerly point on Earth, these scientists are learning more about the ozone layer. They also study the Antarctic ice cap, to see if it is being affected by global warming.

Above the southern continent

Earth is protected from some of the Sun's harmful rays by a layer of gas high in the atmosphere, called ozone. In recent years a hole has appeared in the ozone layer over Antarctica, the frozen continent around the South Pole. Scientists believe that the ozone was partly attacked by gases called CFCs, which can be used in aerosol sprays, refrigerators and fast-food packages. The countries of the world have agreed to reduce the use of these gases. If the ozone hole gets much bigger, Antarctic animals such as seals and penguins might be damaged. Temperatures would probably rise and some of the frozen continent's ice would start to melt. This could affect all the other continents.

Into the future

The continents will always go on changing, but most of the changes will be gradual and take place over many years. Some of the changes will be due to natural forces, such as the movement of Earth's **plates**. Others will be due to the actions of humans, using up Earth's natural **resources**. We also use more and more land on all the continents, making it difficult for some animals and plants to survive. We must hope that the world's people will work together to make future changes positive and valuable.

Continent facts and figures

Size of continents and their largest countries

continent	area in sq km	area in sq miles	largest country	area in sq km	area in sq miles
Asia	44,614,000	17,225,562	China*	9,572,900	3,696,117
Africa	30,216,000	11,631,714	Sudan	2,503,900	966,761
North America	24,230,000	9,355,255	Canada	9,976,100	3,851,794
South America	17,814,000	6,878,024	Brazil	8,456,500	3,265,073
Antarctica	14,245,000	5,500,025	—	—	—
Europe	10,505,000	4,056,003	Ukraine*	603,700	233,090
Oceania	8,503,000	3,283,027	Australia	7,682,300	2,966,153

*Russia (partly in Europe and Asia) is the biggest country in the world
(21,347,100 sq km/8,442,162 sq miles).

Population of continents and their most populous countries

continent	pop in millions	country	pop in millions
Asia	3672	China	1285
Africa	794	Nigeria	112
Europe	727	Germany*	82
North America	487	USA	278
South America	346	Brazil	170
Oceania	31	Australia	19

*Russia (part of which is in Europe) has a population of 147 million.

Growth of population

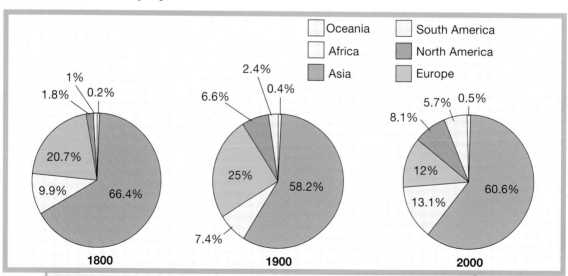

> These charts show the percentage of the world's
> people in six continents in 1800, 1900 and 2000.
> Antarctica has stayed at zero.

Most populous cities

continent	city	country	pop in millions
Asia	Tokyo	Japan	26.4
North America	Mexico City	Mexico	18.1
South America	São Paulo	Brazil	18.0
Europe	Paris	France	9.6
Africa	Cairo	Egypt	9.5
Oceania	Sydney	Australia	3.8

Worst earthquakes of the 20th century

location	country	continent	date	number of people killed
Tangshan	China	Asia	1976	242,000
Xining	China	Asia	1927	200,000
Gansu	China	Asia	1920	180,000
Tokyo	Japan	Asia	1923	143,000
Messina	Italy	Europe	1908	100,000
Gansu	China	Asia	1932	80,000
Yungay	Peru	S. America	1970	67,000
Quetta	Pakistan	Asia	1935	50,000
Roudhon	Iran	Asia	1990	40,000
Armenia	Armenia	Asia	1988	25,000

As this busy street suggests, Tokyo in Japan has the highest population of any city in the world.

Glossary

adapt to change in order to suit the conditions

ancestor person who lived long ago from whom someone is descended

climate weather conditions in a particular area

coast edge of land where it meets the sea

continental margin whole region of the continental shelf, slope and rise

continental rise gently sloping pile of sand and mud at the edge of a continental slope, leading to the deep ocean

continental shelf area of gently sloping seabed at the edge of a continent, where the water is shallow

continental slope steep slope at the edge of a continental shelf, further out to sea

crust hard outer layer of Earth

delta fan-shaped area at the mouth of some rivers, where the river splits into many smaller channels

desert area of very dry land

earthquake sudden shaking of the ground caused by movements beneath Earth's surface

equator imaginary circle that stretches around the middle of Earth

fault crack in Earth's crust

habitat natural environment, or home, of an animal or plant

hominid one of several different kinds of human-like creatures that existed on Earth before modern humans

hunter-gatherer wandering person who lives by hunting, fishing and collecting wild food such as roots and berries

igneous (of rocks) made from cooled, solidified lava or magma

Industrial Revolution rapid development of machinery and factories that began in the late 18th century

lava hot molten rock that pours out of a volcano on to Earth's surface

magma hot molten rock formed beneath Earth's surface

metamorphic (of rocks) changed by great heat or pressure

mineral natural, solid substance that is found in Earth's surface

molten melted (turned into liquid by heat)

plate huge piece of Earth's crust

population total number of people who live in a particular place

rainforest thick forest found in warm tropical areas of heavy rainfall

reptile scaly-skinned, cold-blooded animal; snakes, lizards and crocodiles are all reptiles

resource supply of something that can be used

seabed ground under the sea; the ocean floor

sedimentary (of rocks) formed from rock particles that have been moved and laid down by ice, water or wind

settlement place where people live permanently

species type, or kind of animal or plant

steppe flat, grassy plain (especially in Russia)

strata layers of rock

volcano opening where molten rock and gas come from deep inside Earth, often forming a mountain

Further reading

Continents in Close-Up series, Keith Lye and Malcolm Porter (Cherrytree Books, 2000)

Discovering Geography: Volcanoes and Earthquakes, Rebecca Hunter (Raintree, 2003)

The Kingfisher Book of Planet Earth, Martin Redfern (Kingfisher Books, 1999)

The Picture Atlas of the World (Dorling Kindersley, 1998)

Rocks and Minerals: Igneous Rocks, Melissa Stewart (Heinemann Library, 2002)

Mapping Earthforms: Oceans and Seas, Catherine Chambers (Heinemann Library, 2000)

Index

Africa 4, 5, 8, 9, 13, 15,
    16, 18, 21, 24, 25,
    28, 29
animals and plants
    14–17, 27
Antarctica 4, 8, 14, 16,
    18, 27, 28
Asia 4, 5, 8, 12, 13, 16,
    17, 21, 22, 23, 25, 28,
    29
Australia 4, 5, 14–15,
    16, 19

Bangladesh 22

changing continents
    26–7
climate 16, 19, 26
coastlines 10, 12, 26
continental drift 8
continental margin 13
continental plates 7, 8
continental rise 13
continental shelf 12, 13
continental slope 12
countries 4, 24, 28
cyclones and typhoons
    22

deserts 16, 17, 25, 26
dinosaurs 14

earthquakes 9, 23, 29
Earth's crust 6, 9, 10, 13
Earth's plates 6–7, 8, 9,
    10, 13, 23, 27
erosion 11
Eurasia 5
Europe 4, 5, 8, 12, 17,
    21, 24, 25, 28, 29

farming 20, 25
floods 22, 26
forests 16, 17
formation of continents
    5, 6–9

global warming 26, 27
Gondwanaland 8, 14
Great Rift Valley 13

habitats 16–17
hominids 18
humans, early 18–19
hunter-gatherers 19, 20
hurricanes 22

igneous rocks 10

kangaroos and koalas 15

Lake Victoria 21
landscapes 10–13
Laurasia 8
lava 11
linked continents 5

magma 7, 9, 10
metamorphic rocks 11
minerals 10
monkeys 15
mountains 5, 9, 10, 12

natural disasters 22–3
natural resources 21,
    24–5, 27
North America 4, 5, 8,
    16, 17, 19, 20, 21, 22,
    23, 24, 25, 28, 29

Oceania (Australasia) 4,
    5, 8, 23, 25, 28, 29
occanic plates 7
oceans 5, 6, 7, 8, 9, 11,
    13
oil 25
ozone layer 27

Pangaea 8, 12
population explosion 21,
    28
populations 20–1, 28, 29

rainforests 16, 17
rocks 7, 9, 10–11

sea levels 19, 26
sedimentary rocks 10
settlements 18–21
South America 4, 5, 8, 9,
    14, 15, 16, 17, 19, 21,
    23, 24, 25, 28, 29
strata 10
supercontinent 8, 14

towns and cities 4, 20,
    21, 29

volcanoes 6, 7, 9, 11, 23

water resources 21, 24

Titles in the Landscapes and People series include:

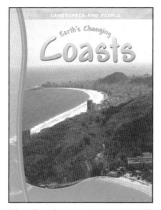

Hardback   1 844 21392 7

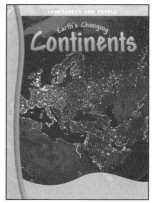

Hardback   1 844 21393 5

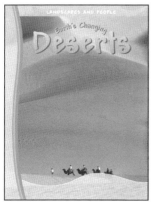

Hardback   1 844 21394 3

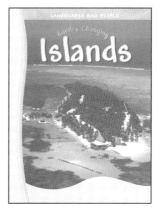

Hardback   1 844 21395 1

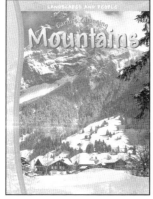

Hardback   1 844 21396 X

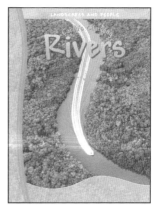

Hardback   1 844 21397 8

Find out about the other titles in this series on our website www.raintreepublishers.co.uk